MW01296008

Daily Affirmations for Success & Happiness

500 Positive Affirmations to Rewire Your Brain

By Creed McGregor

Disclaimer

The information provided in this book is meant to provide helpful information on the subjects discussed. The publisher and author are not responsible for any financial or health needs that may require professional supervision and are not liable for any damages or negative consequences from any treatment, action, application or preparation to any person reading or following the information provided in this book. References are provided for informational purposes only and do not constitute endorsement of any websites or other sources.

Copyright© 2016 Maddog Publications All rights reserved. No part of this publication may be reproduced, distributed, or transmitted in any form or by any means including photocopying, recording, or other electronic or mechanical methods without prior written permission of the publisher and author. Except in the case of brief quotations embodied in critical reviews and certain other non-commercial uses permitted by copyright law.

While attempts have been made to verify that the information contained in this book is accurate, neither the publisher nor author assumes any responsibility for errors, omissions, interpretations, or usage of the subject matters herein.

This publication contains the opinions and ideas of its author and is intended for informational purposes only. Neither the publisher nor author shall in any event be held liable for any loss damages incurred from the usage of this publication.

Introduction

Your thoughts can be used for good or bad without even realizing it. Unfortunately, most of what we see and hear today is negative. News, media, music, coworkers, and even family members can spread negative thoughts with no direct intention. When our minds are taking in negative information, that becomes our thoughts and our thoughts become our actions.

Scientists tell us that our thoughts generate unique frequencies that attract back to us like frequencies. This is known as the Law of Attraction. This universal law states that we generate the things, events, and people that appear in our lives. Our thoughts, feelings, words, and actions produce energies (unique frequency) that attract like energies. Negative energies attract negative energies and positive energies attract positive energies.

This means nothing happens in our lives by coincidence. You attract everything into your life, everything that happens to you, through your thoughts, feelings, words, and actions. Notice that this chain of events begins with your thoughts.

Knowing this will make it easier to understand why having negative thoughts of depression, anger, hatred, greed, or selfishness to name a few, can bring you more of the same.

By learning to directly control your thoughts, you are able to block out negative energies. This can be accomplished by thinking only positive thoughts. Positive thinking is a theory that many ancient masters and philosophers have used throughout history.

Successful men and women have used positive thinking to inspire thousands. Many teachers and motivational speakers today use the power of positive thinking to help change people's lives for the better. This positive thinking technique is easier said than done however.

To think positively you have to concentrate on your thoughts, especially at first. The minute your subconscious mind takes over, it can fall back into old habits of negative thinking. Practicing to think positive all day long will take some effort considering we have 35-48 thoughts per minute. Being persistent in regard to thinking positively will eventually become a habit and a new way of life.

You will start to notice good things happening to you. You'll notice things seem to fall into place and go your way. Do not dismiss this phenomenon as a mere coincidence. It is great powers at work. The more evidence you obtain that it's working, the easier it will become to master. Before you know it, you'll be living the life you've always dreamed of. A life of success and happiness anyone would appreciate.

500 Affirmations for Success and Happiness

To begin controlling your thoughts, you can recite affirmations. You can read them quietly to yourself or aloud, it makes no difference. Reading these affirmations will begin to rewire your brain for success and happiness. Take some time each day to read as many as you can. Read them slowly and concentrate on their meaning. The more feeling you express the better results you will achieve.

Many find it best to start their day with affirmations but they can be read anytime. If you find yourself feeling negative during the day, they can help get you back on track. Even reading them at night prior to bed can have a wonderful effect. Read them as often as possible.

Your mind will begin to believe what it is hearing. This will flow through into your words and actions. Positive energies will then have no choice but to gravitate into your life. Start now, read them often, and make positive thinking a habit to attract the success and happiness you deserve.

"Happiness does not depend on what you have or who you are. It solely relies on what you think." Gautama Buddha

I am in charge of my life

I attract success in whatever I do

Success finds me no matter what

I embrace only positive thoughts

I am responsible for my own life

I control my thoughts

I change negative thoughts into positive thoughts

I pursue my dreams with ease

I can achieve anything I desire

I always find a way to succeed

I overcome obstacles with ease

I am happier now than I have ever been

My happiness is contagious

Success is abundant in my life

I take on challenges with confidence

I am a winner because I choose to be

I achieve massive success

I believe in my self one hundred percent

I do not fear failure

My eyes are open to opportunity

I am more successful than ever

I create my own success and happy life

My happiness helps me to succeed

I am happy to be alive today

I look forward to the challenges of each
day

I explore my dreams to achieve success

I enjoy every minute of my life

I maximize my brain's ability to adapt

I work hard towards success

I am strong and brave

I achieve happiness by my own thoughts

My success is a journey

I believe in my actions and myself

I have the power to live a happy life

Everything I do brings me happiness

I can find a solution to any problem

I make my life what I want it to be

I'm gleaming with happiness and joy

Being happy is my favorite thing to do

I am so happy it rubs off on others

I wake up each day excited for opportunity

I wake up ready to achieve my dreams

I believe therefore I can achieve

I am successful because I don't quit

I utilize my passions to achieve anything

My future is what I perceive it to be

I have no fears of the future

My confidence is soaring

I stand up for my beliefs

My ability to master my challenges is
limitless

I retain the virtues needed to be
successful

I deserve to be as successful as anyone

It is my right to be happy and successful

My happiness is more abundant each day

I am bursting with energy and brimming
with joy

I have no regrets of the past

I tackle each day with courage and
bravery

My road is carved to greatness

I radiate beauty, charm and happiness

I look at every situation with great
optimism

My days are always very productive

I'm relaxed, calm and peaceful

I am helpful to others whenever I can be

I have many things I am grateful for

My generosity is unique and unselfish

I'm open-minded to positive suggestions

Small daily tasks brings me joy

I am cheerful about the future

I do not fear failure

I attempt things that used to scare me

I'm cheerful, joyous and free

My successful thinking is consistent

I dress for success everyday

I am worth all that has come to me

I am respectful and courteous to all around me

My cheerfulness spills onto others

I enjoy smiling and making others smile

I take joy in everything I do

My cheerful mood gets me through
anything

Life is what I choose to make it

I love having the opportunity to be
successful

I am completely satisfied with who I am
today

My social skills help me to be successful

I am deserving of a happy and wonderful
life

Nothing bothers me because I don't let it

I avoid negativity at all costs

I am the master of my feelings and
emotions

I am grateful and thankful for abundance

I carve my own path to happiness

My accomplishments far out weigh my failures

My ambitions carve a path to success

Today I am compassionate and empathetic

My exuberant attitude is unrestrained

I willingly share what I have with others

I help those in need whenever possible

My diligence and persistence sees a job to the end

I am capable of fitting a particular situation

I have great intuition and instinctive knowledge

I'm inspired daily to succeed

Nothing can stop me from being happy

My thoughts sculpt a positive attitude towards life

I am one with the universe and open my arms to its energy

Success comes to me through positive energies

I am good at what I do for a living and climb to the top

My determination to succeed is unmatched

Only I decide the level of my own success

No person or thing can determine my success

Nobody but me controls my happiness

I wake up with more than enough energy to succeed each day

My smile reveals my level of happiness and success

I smile at everyone so they can pick up on my positive energies

Opportunity is everywhere I look

I love taking on and overcoming challenges

I understand challenges make me stronger

With every challenge I conquer the stronger I become

I soak up all the positive energies around me

I have a force field against negative energies

My soul and spirit are tuned into positive frequencies

When I want to accomplish something I do it with precision

I am grateful for the gifts life brings me

I have not felt this good in my entire life

I can conquer any task that is put before me

I never fail because I never quit

Persistence is the key to my achievements

I am on top of the world and nothing can knock me down

When I do falter I get right back at it like nothing happened

I am not controlled by fear or rejection

I never stop moving closer to my goals
each day

The universe brings me more happiness
than I have ever had

I achieve large goals by working on them
daily

I release my goals to the universe and ask
for help

I concentrate and focus on my most
important goals

My goals are written out and I read them
everyday

I dare not live a day without a clear goal
in mind

I have complete faith in my abilities to
accomplish my goals

I set goals with clear intentions to achieve
them

I do not go about my day without first
focusing on my goals

I start each day with a clear path of
intention

I do not just stagger my way through life anymore

I have clear-cut goals that will be achieved by a specific deadline

All my goals have deadlines to help me stay on track

My success is measured by the amount of goals I intend to accomplish

Success is the journey towards my goals

After I achieve a goal I set another one to take its place

No one can stop me from achieving what I want

My passion to achieve great things is stronger than ever

I will let everyone know through my actions that I am successful

My actions are a direct result of my thinking and words

I realize every positive direction is started by a positive thought

I think positive, I speak positive, and I act positive

No negative force can penetrate my positive energy field

I am in tune with the universe and all the gifts it brings me

I think a thought with intentions of doing some good

I purposely do not think negative thoughts

I do not allow circumstances to control my life

I create circumstances on purpose to fulfill my dreams

I am a success today because those are my intentions

I cannot fail because I will not quit

Success is the measurement of how hard I am working towards my goals

Being focused is being driven by a greater power

I am successful no matter what the results may be

My effort is what makes me successful

I cannot fail if I know I cannot fail

I achieve happiness by being purposeful in all I do

I know being happy means being driven by purpose

I am driven by purpose to achieve my goals and this creates my happiness

Happiness is what happens when I get after a goal

My life has meaning and I have meaning

Whatever my purpose I have faith I will find it

I am happy every single day that I choose to be, what a wonderful feeling

Happiness cannot escape me unless I take my eye off my daily goals

Where I used to feel empty I now feel full of life

I put myself first because otherwise I am
no good to anyone
Life is only difficult when I make it
difficult

I do not bathe in self-pity anymore

If I fall I get back up and carry on, no big
deal

To achieve a purposeful goal is pure joy

I believe I am here for a reason and that
reason is not to be unhappy

I can simply smile to bring my mood back
to where it should be

I'm aware I might fall once in a while so I
can do it more gracefully

Failure does not occur until I quit trying

I learn from my failure so I can achieve
success that much quicker

Success is a measure of my goal focus

Success is not after I achieve a goal, but
rather on my journey towards it

I am successful only when I choose to be

I am happy only when I choose to be

Today I choose to be both happy and successful

Challenges make me stronger

I treat every challenge like a learning experience to success

Challenges are like the weights of success building

I use challenges to strengthen who I am

With every challenge comes another round of success

The bigger the challenge the bigger the reward of overcoming it

I take on challenges without fear or thought of not conquering it

Obstacles do not make me mad but bring me joy that I may grow from them

Obstacles and challenges let me know I'm on the right track

My life is what I make of it each day

When I am focused I am happy and successful

Positive thoughts pave my road to success

The road of positive thought can have potholes but I just avoid them

I know I do not need to be a genius to be successful

Anybody can be a success if that is what they choose

I choose to be successful today and this is my thinking each morning

My positive energies attract more of the same

My vibrations and frequencies bring me the gifts of life

No matter what it is I want I know I can have it

When I am feeling down I bring myself back up with positive thought

When necessary I will go somewhere quiet and purposefully think positive

When I control my own thoughts I control
my own life

I believe thinking is something that
should be focused

I do not let my thinking go off on its own

I govern my thinking to benefit itself

My mind does not accept negative
thoughts

I block out all negative frequencies and
energies

I control my level of happiness with my
thought thermostat

I can adjust the level of comfort in my life
with how I am thinking

I do not let my thoughts venture away
from my goals

I am the creator of my own universe

I choose to be where I am today simply by
how I think

I am the most successful person I know

I cannot fail when I choose to do otherwise

My soul is bubbling over with happiness

Happiness sings and dances around on my spirit

My life is no more than making a decision to be happy

My happiness gauge is always on full

I am happy because my thoughts are happy

I take the time I need to make the right decision

I trust my instincts to do what is right

I am guided by my intuition and will not fail

Listening to my inner voice I am able to react confidently

No decision I make is without meaning

Every choice I decide upon is full of gut instinct

When I know I am listening to myself I know I will succeed

Failure is an option but I choose not to partake

If doubt throws a party I throw a bigger party of confidence

When in doubt I ask myself why and then listen

There is a lot to be said about doubt but I don't hear it

When my mind is made up that I will succeed there is no other option

I love the choices life gives me daily

I do not frown upon circumstances that are not of my liking

I ask myself why these are my circumstances and then I make new ones

I do not dwell about things not going my way

I have complete faith everything happens for a reason

To be happy brings joy to everyone
around me

Happiness is contagious so I wear it with
a smile

I live simply and laugh often

Laughter is the measurement of
happiness

I laugh whenever I get a chance

Laughing emits positive energies that
attract like energies

To laugh is to live and what better way to
express my happiness

A laugh is like a smile times 100

The more feelings of happiness I have the
more I get in return

When I am happy, I am the person I am
supposed to be

I do onto others as I wish they do onto me

I do not expect more from someone than
what I am giving them

Life is only as fair as I make it

To be happy I don't have to do much
other than make a choice to be

Happiness is only a decision I can make

To think happy is to feel happy is to be
happy

I am winning because I choose not to lose

A happy me is a successful me is a happy
me

I understand what comes around goes
around so I spread joy

I reap what I sow so I choose to sow seeds
of joy

What may seem like a setback actually
propels me forward

I take from every experience all that I can

Every experience and opportunity makes
me stronger

Each person I meet enhances my spirit in
some meaningful way

I know nothing can happen without the
help of other people

I attract the type of positive person that I strive to be

People in my life help lift my spirits and give me hope

Happiness can hide in many forms so I look for it in everything

I become what I think about is a rule I live by

The universe holds all the answers to any questions I might ask

I nourish my body with healthy foods and thoughts alike

I do not get complacent or stop moving forward

Even in the face of adversity I come out better than I was

I take in and learn from adversity and hardships

I do not believe in being depressed or meaningless

I am here for a reason and have faith that I am on the right track

I will always be the best person I can be

I treat others with the same respect I wish
to have

I am honest in every aspect of my life

To hurt others is a sin I refuse to commit

I am only as good as I choose to be so I set
the bar high

I hurdle challenges like an Olympic
champion

To take me down I would have to give in
and that will never happen

I have the ability to focus and attack a
goal like a hungry lion

I am ever so patient when looking for the
right opportunity

Opportunity strikes all around me

I take advantage of opportunities the
universe presents to me

Nothing is put in front of me for no reason

I learn what I can from every life experience no matter how big or small

Opportunity is frequent when I am open to it

Nothing happens in life without first having an opportunity

I move with precise accuracy when preying on an opportunity

What I do today will directly affect what happens to me tomorrow

I am not perfect and every day brings new opportunities

I do not get down on myself when I do not meet my own expectations

Try, try, and try again and I will not fail

What I see now is all the good around me at any given moment

I've learned to love all aspects of life

I radiate the frequency of love knowing it is a powerful force

I believe everything is put in front of me to strengthen my spirit in some way

The more I succeed the easier it becomes

Being happy is a habit I cannot easily break

When I look for the joy in everything I seem to find it

I keep my eyes and ears and mind open to new opportunities

Knowing how to react in any situation is easier when I'm full of joy

I never react to a situation without first applying positive thought

When my intentions are good things always work out

If I always think positive I don't have to struggle with negativity

I surround myself with other positive people

So many people in my life are supportive and encouraging

It's so easy to see the good in people when I look for it

The people in my life help me to achieve success

The key to unlocking life is happiness and joy

When I'm happy I'm in tune with the universe

I do not question why things happen

I respond appropriately when I'm questioned

I always know exactly what to say in any situation

I help others with comforting words when necessary

I'm there for people that need someone for support

I do not sway from what I know is right

I believe in myself no matter the situation

Success cannot elude me because I attract it

The forces that rule will always benefit me when I'm acting on positivity

I attract money, success, and abundance into my life

I gravitate towards other like-minded people

I believe we only meet those who were put in front of us for a reason

If I consider all the opportunities around me, I have no shortage of prospects

My thoughts bring the material things that I want into my life

I succeed through tenacity, dedication, perseverance, and faith

For what might have seemed impossible to me is not anymore

I can have anything I desire and it will be well deserved

I share my knowledge of life with good intentions to others

I can succeed today simply because it is possible

I deserve to be rich, successful, and happy as much as anyone else

Success does not have limits other than
how I think

If I want to succeed I can and if I want to
be happy I can be that as well

If character measures a person I'm in luck

I am the best version of me that I can be
and I try hard at it

I do not get frustrated at change but
rather welcome its entrance

I do not get lost when I am not sure the
way, I simply ask for help

The key to happiness lies within our spirit

I find happiness each day in the smallest
things

When I am happy for other's success it
brings me the same

The key to success is being grateful for
what I have

I am grateful for everything in my life and
things still to come

I am grateful for the opportunities that
have yet shown themselves to me

I am powerful beyond measure and I am careful with that power

I am the most brilliant, talented, and fabulous person I know

I know my playing small does not serve others

I do all I can to serve and help others along the way

I stand up for my beliefs and do not easily deter from them

I am always open-minded to new ideas and philosophies

I take calculated risks without fear or hesitation

I am a better person today than I was yesterday

I am always growing in a positive direction

Whenever I learn a lesson I grow from it

I become a more successful person every single day

Without fear of rejection I have reached new levels of success

I am not afraid to be myself

I do not look down on myself when faced with rejection

I am not intimidated by seemingly difficult tasks

I am grateful for my health, success, and abundance

When I believe in myself good things happen

My confidence is unshaken and remains solid in adversity

I become stronger in the face of adversity

I make critical decision making seem easy

I trust in my decisions and stick by them

I have to have faith in my choices, if I don't I begin to question myself

My faith is solid even under the most severe of situations

I look for the good in every outcome

Success is partly seeing the good in all
deals and transactions

Success is not partial to any one person; it
comes to all whom ask for it

I ask for success each day through
intentional positive thinking

Success comes my way just as freely as
the oxygen I breath

To be successful I am constantly shifting
my thoughts to attracting it

I love whom I am when I am striving
towards a worthwhile goal

To remain happy I continually monitor
my thoughts

The universe brings to me the success I
demand of it

I refuse to be a burden to anyone

I take full responsibility of my own life

As a human being I am responsible for all
of my actions

I am careful what I think because those thoughts become my actions

I started taking control of my life when I started taking control of my thoughts

I think positive therefore I receive back positive

Love is a high frequency that I try to radiate at all times

I am glowing with the frequency of love at this very moment

I know I cannot fail if I remain positive in all that I do

I never doubt my abilities therefore they are never a problem

Most of what I used to worry about never happened

I will not waste my time worrying about things that likely won't happen anyway

I recognize all negative energies so I can remove them quickly

When all I think is positive that is all I get back

I often reflect on all the great things I have
in my life

I am grateful for the smallest details in my
life as well as the largest

I remember where I came from and that I
am a better person every minute

I do not let the past determine who I am
today

I have learned to appreciate all the
intangible things in my life

I let success land where it may then move
towards it

Watching the news is not something I
care to do anymore

Mainstream media is mostly negative and
serves me no good purpose

To be successful I had to change my
thought process

I am a person of interest today because I
am interested in others

I find people intriguing and always ask
myself what attracted them into my life

With positive thought I can accomplish anything

I share my success with others whenever I have an opportunity

I unselfishly give to others because it brings me joy

I ask a lot of questions because that is the only way to get answers

I am here for reasons much larger than myself

I do not think too much on what could have been

I am happy being around friends and family

I am happy surrounding myself with loved ones

I feed off the energy of other happy and successful people

Staying positive is my force field against negative energies

I can only achieve what I set out to accomplish

I am not afraid to take on new things

Doing something I've never done before helps me grow in character

I have all the knowledge I need to be a success

When I feel I am not good enough I remember the universe does not discriminate

Those whom ask shall receive and that's all there is to it good or bad

I am careful what I wish because it will most likely come true

I only read, watch and listen to positive stories

There is no room in my life for negativity or the things it brings

I steer clear of negative people with all due respect

I do not criticize those who think differently than I do, it is their choice

We all have choices and my choices are success and happiness

Being happy breeds success

If success is a trick I guess I'm a magician

Nothing eludes me that can make me more successful

I radiate success because I can't help it

Never again will I be less successful than I am right now

I am always moving in a forward positive direction

I know the road to success and all of its shortcuts

For me success is like looking for an address, I eventually find it if I don't give up

I know the only way for me to fail is to stop trying

If I never give up I will always succeed no matter what it is I'm pursuing

Life became successful for me once I changed my thinking

My happiness is really nothing more than a frame of mind

I live to laugh and laugh to live

Knowing that I am as successful as I want
to be is a huge burden off my shoulders

I am large and in charge of my thoughts
and my life

Life is what I think it to be

I succeed at things because that is my
attitude going in

I have so many happy thoughts a day they
spillover to the next day

My mind is set each morning that I will
succeed that day

Without thought control I am a pinball to
circumstance

I make my own life by making choices to
think only good things

My thoughts are always in rhythm with
my goals

I deter from thinking anything that
reflects negativity

To have good things happen to me I have
to think good things

If I'm honest, only positive thoughts feel
normal to me

Thinking negative goes against every
fiber of my being

I'm a productive human being when I'm in
a positive frame of mind

To know myself is to know all measures
of success

I can say I am completely happy the
person I am today

I can only improve when I work on myself

I don't try to change others I only set by
example

I am kind and considerate to everyone I
meet

I stand with pride and confidence when
shaking hands with someone

I look people in the eyes when meeting
them

I am proud to be me and no one can take
that away

When I reach a new level of success I
always reflect on what got me there

What used to seem unachievable is now
within grasp

I have succeeded in everything I have
attempted to do

I will not waiver from thinking positive
ever again

It is my faith that carves the path to my
success

All is the way it should be when my
thoughts are worthy

If I can help someone that asks for help I
am more than happy to

My spirit is glowing with happiness more
than ever

I have so much faith that all things good
for me will come

To know me is to know pure happiness

I show the world how happy I can really
be

Me being happy with my life is a
testament to positive thinking

I do not let others control what happens
to me

I make my own circumstances by
attracting positive frequencies

No harm can come to my family or me
when I am thinking only good

Now that I know the key to success, I will
not stop striving forward

My soul is full of pure joy and nothing can
take that from me

I have tears in my eyes for all I have
suffered but I am grateful for life's lessons

I respect life and the universe and do not
try to take advantage

I only think upon positive things for me
and for others

I achieve the amount of success I wish to

Believing in myself has given me new
hope and happiness

Success is mirrored by my thoughts

I cannot control the thoughts of others
nor is it my place

I only practice self-development and self-
success

I do not worry about what others do; it is
their own making

I focus on my own development because
that is what matters most

I learn from others and take away what I
can from all situations

I stop once in awhile to smell the roses
and enjoy life

My life is what I make it and only what I
make it

I have learned more about myself by
monitoring my thoughts

Everything positive in my life is directly
from a positive thought

My love for life is apparent to everyone
because I do not hide it

I am grateful for my happy and healthy
spirit

I send my love out to the universe
through my feelings of gratefulness

The person I am today is a better person
than yesterday

I read affirmations everyday to achieve
continued success and happiness

Thank you for reading! I know success
and happiness will find its way to you.

If you enjoyed this book I'd like to ask you
for a favor. Would you be kind enough to
leave a review for this book on Amazon? I
would greatly appreciate it and thanks
again!

The End